SISKIYOU COUNTY LIBRARY

3 2871 0020243

D0437246

IDENTIFYING

SNAKES

The new compact study guide and identifier

Nigel Marven and Rob Harvey

IDENTIFYING

i

SNAKES

The new compact study guide and identifier

Nigel Marven and Rob Harvey

59.96

cop. 2

CHARTWELL
BOOKS, INC.

SISKIYOU COUNTY PUBLIC LIBRARY
719 FOURTH STREET
YREKA, CALIFORNIA 96097

A QUINTET BOOK

Published by Chartwell Books
A Division of Book Sales, Inc.
114 Northfield Avenue
Edison, New Jersey 08837

This edition produced for sale in the U.S.A., its
territories and dependencies only.

Copyright © 1996 Quintet Publishing Limited.
All rights reserved. No part of this publication
may be reproduced, stored in a retrieval system
or transmitted in any form or by any means,
electronic, mechanical, photocopying, recording
or otherwise, without the permission of the
copyright holder.

ISBN 0-7858-0371-8

This book was designed and produced by
Quintet Publishing Limited
6 Blundell Street
London N7 9BH

Creative Director: Richard Dewing
Designer: Mike Head
Project Editor: Anna Briffa
Editor: Geraldine Christy

Typeset in Great Britain by
Central Southern Typesetters, Eastbourne
Manufactured in China by
Regent Publishing Services Ltd
Printed in China by Leefung-Asco Printers Ltd

PICTURE CREDITS

S. C. Bisserôt: 66(t), (b), 67(t), (b)
Jenny Daltry: 15(t), 55(t), 56, 65(b)
Jeff Gee: 15(b), 26(b), 31, 40(b), 53(b), 61, 78(b)
Nigel Marven: 13, 28(t), 46(b), 50(t).
Papilio/Robert Pickett: 17(b), 28(t), 42, 68, 76
Andrew Shillabeer: 5, 6, 11, 12, 14, 16, 17(t), 18, 19,
20, 21(t), 22(t), (b), 24, 28(b), 30, 32(b), 33, 34, 35(t),
(b), 37, 38(t), (b), 39(t), (b), 40(t), 41, 43(t), 65(t), 69,
70, 71(b), 72, 73(b), 74, 75(t), 78(t), 79.
John Weigel: 10, 23, 25, 26(t), 27, 29(t), (b), 54(t), (b),
57(t), (b), 59(t), (b), 60(t), (b), 63(b), 64, 77(t), 77(b).

CONTENTS

INTRODUCTION

We think snakes are the most splendid of animals, though their alien form, so different from that of human beings, is loathsome to many people. They are successful predators who have pioneered elegant strategies to turn leglessness to their advantage. Some of them can catch a bat in mid air, even in the pitch dark. Others can climb among the thinnest of twigs, stretching and contorting their bodies into superb, geometric designs. There are some that are so strong that it takes three men or more to unwind their coils from around the trunk of a tree.

Being "snake fans" we also marvel at the diversity of their exquisite patterns and colours. There are over 2,700 species ranging in size from 10mm to 10 metres (½in to 33 feet). Here we can only show you some of our favourites, but we hope this selection may inspire others to become interested in snakes.

WHAT IS A SNAKE?

Snakes are members of the class Reptilia together with lizards, crocodilians and turtles. All these reptiles have waterproof skins covered in scales or horny plates that can be modified to make elaborate crests or spines, or transformed into toughened armour or protective shells.

The White-lipped Pit Viper belongs to arguably the most advanced group of snakes.

Snakes show the most conservative of reptilian designs. Their streamlined bodies are stripped to the bare essentials and only a few have any adornments at all; some vipers have a horn on their snout and there is a water snake with tentacles, but as snake accoutrements go, that is about it. To identify one from another it is necessary to look at the marvellous patterns and colours of the skin, as well as subtle differences in shape and size. There are some species of snake so similar, that to tell them apart one must count the exact number of scales at specific points on the body.

Outside appearances may vary; a turtle is very different from a snake, for example, but on the inside all reptiles have an important feature in common. Unlike mammals and birds they do not have an internal heating system that allows them to maintain a constant body temperature. To keep active reptiles must rely on external sources of warmth, so if air temperatures are not high enough to keep them up to speed, they must bask in the sun. Under these conditions if you can watch a snake or lizard for long enough you will see it shuttling between sun and shade to keep its body at just the right temperature.

In the tropics it is so warm that reptiles can function for much of the time, but in temperate climates cool weather forces them to remain torpid in their retreats and they must hibernate during the winter.

Another feature that defines a reptile is that their embryos are enclosed within eggs, although some snakes and lizards may seem to give birth. Those able to do this retain their eggs within their bodies – becoming a sort of mobile incubator, until development is complete and they produce a litter of babies.

HOW SNAKES AROSE

When it comes to legless reptiles the snakes are not an exclusive club. Many lizards, some skinks, slowworms and the Australian Flap Footed lizards have lost or nearly lost their limbs. But why? These lizards are either burrowers or denizens of confined spaces. In a tunnel anything that sticks out from the body can snag and hinder movement, so it is much easier to be a "smoothie" and do without legs. In all probability the first snakes evolved as legless creatures to be efficient burrowers.

Snakes have also lost their external ears and the ability to hear most airborne sounds. Instead the bones in their head are modified to detect vibrations, vitally important underground. A burrowing origin also led to snakes having their glassy, unblinking stare. They do not have eyelids, so can never shut their eyes, even when they are sleeping, but there is a tough transparent spectacle that protects the eye from damage when the snake is pushing through soil or dense vegetation. The prototype snake designed for a subterranean lifestyle probably arose from a lizard or lizard-like reptile. There are even some snakes that show direct evidence of an ancestor with limbs; the giant boas and pythons have tiny spurs at the base of the tail, the vestiges of legs. Many scientists think monitor lizards are the closest living relatives of snakes. Like them they have a deeply forked tongue for sampling odours in the air and the ability to swallow large items of food. The ancestral stock of snakes may have looked very similar to these giant lizards. Whatever may have happened 120 million years ago, the first snakes soon expanded their empire above ground and set about colonizing the world, using skills unique to themselves.

MOVING AROUND

At the surface snakes had to find effective ways of locomotion without the use of legs. They do this in three main ways:

1. "Squirming" or Serpentine movement
Muscular waves undulate the snake's body in a series of S shaped curves and it propels itself forwards by levering the hind part of each curve against the irregularities in the ground. Snakes swim by pushing the curves against the resistance of the water.

2. "Caterpillar Crawl" or "Rectilinear Creeping"
A technique used by stout, heavy snakes such as pythons and vipers. They move slowly forwards by pushing groups of belly scales against the ground while sliding others forwards, giving the general impression of the whole body gliding in a straight line.

3. "Sidewinding"
Some snakes that live on shifting sand have a spectacular mode of travel. The snake

1

2

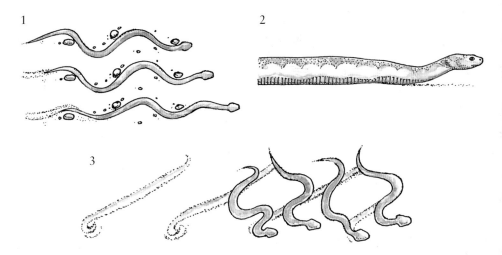

3

throws out a lateral arc with its head and the front part of its body; while transferring the rest of its bulk to this forward purchase, it throws out another loop, and by repeating this process it moves sideways in a series of steps.

SNAKE FEEDING

There are no vegetarian snakes; they are all carnivorous. It seems that for every type of animal food, whether frog spawn, spiders, slugs, rodents, birds, lizard eggs, even antelopes, there is a snake somewhere that is able to eat it.

These reptiles would seem to be at a disadvantage to other predators that can run and jump, but their thin bodies can be an asset. Have you ever seen a cat that could follow a mouse right into its burrow? Snakes have no claws for overpowering and tearing up prey but they have developed techniques that are uniquely their own. Some have a venomous bite and they all

have the ability to swallow an item of food that exceeds the diameter of their heads. If it is a food that cannot fight back, it can simply be grabbed and held with the snake's inwardly curved teeth. These are useless for chewing, so the food must be swallowed whole. The bones in a snake jaw are joined by muscles and ligaments; this flexibility and elasticity allows a huge gape and ability to swallow larger items of food. The teeth are alternately freed and refastened and the food is dragged into the gullet. Then the neck muscles are brought into play, forcing the meal towards the stomach. The snake's skin is so flexible that it can be stretched without tearing if the food is really large. Really bulky prey can take a long time to swallow but the snake does not choke as it has a reinforced windpipe that can be thrust out of the side of the mouth, allowing it to breathe.

Not all prey can be swallowed alive – if it is large enough to cause injury or has

Boomslang: One of Africa's most venomous snakes.

teeth or claws, it must be immobilized first. To do this, snakes have their own specialized techniques. Boas, pythons, king snakes and several others use constriction. After an animal or bird has been grabbed, these snakes quickly throw one or two coils around it, drawing these inexorably tighter, until the prey loses consciousness because it is unable to breathe. The food is not crushed during this process, but is suffocated.

Other snakes can incapacitate prey with a single bite, as they have become living chemical factories specialized to produce toxic fluids. Venoms are modified digestive juices, clear or yellowish liquids whose exact composition varies between species. Some components cause the prey's nervous system to malfunction while others break down muscles and blood vessels. Most venoms cause a multitude of effects that work in concert to paralyse and eventually kill. The snakes store their venom in glands behind each eye that connect with teeth modified for injection. Vipers have the most elaborate fangs; when they are not in use they are folded in the roof of the mouth, but during a strike they swivel forward and venom is forced at high pressure through a duct in the tooth. Members of the cobra family have more simple fixed fangs that are generally shorter than those of vipers as they cannot be folded and stowed away.

Hijacking another creature with chemicals is one of the greatest snake accomplishments. This techniques allows minimum physical contact with potentially dangerous prey. For instance it takes only a fraction of a second for a rattlesnake to strike, inject venom and release its hold. It will then wait or even retreat before tracking the scent trail of the dying animal and eating the body.

Of course, a weapon with the efficacy of venom can also be used in defence. But snakes will only waste this precious resource on larger creatures, including human beings, when they perceive their life is at risk. The rattle of rattlesnakes and the vivid colour of coral snakes are warnings to keep away, so venom can be preserved for getting a meal. A bite in self-defence is always the last resort.

SNAKE COURTSHIP

Perfume is crucial in the courtship of snakes. During the breeding season the females produce a scent trail to draw in a suitor. A female in breeding condition exudes chemical messages or pheromones from her skin, so once a pair have made contact the male checks her out with a frenzy of tongue flicking. Courtship can be perfunctory, but a male can spend several hours using his chin to caress a female before he finally moves his tail beneath hers to mate.

For some species courtship is a highly gregarious affair, and a writhing "snake ball" is the result, with up to 30 males pushing and jostling around a female, until one of them succeeds in mating with her.

The males of some rattlesnakes, vipers and Australian elapids even indulge in bouts of wrestling. These ritualized duels sometimes last for up to an hour as each of the combatants tries to gain the upper hand. The two snakes push and twist, raising their bodies above the ground, as each tries to force its opponent's head to the ground. They fall back repeatedly before trying again. Fatigue forces the weaker, usually smaller, snake to retreat and the victor mates with the female who is

Forest Cobra. Despite being a slender snake, this is Africa's largest cobra.

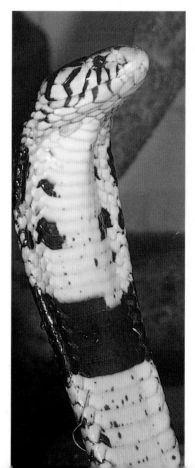

generally nearby, although she seems to take no interest in the combat dance, and could even mate with another passing male while the jousting is in progress.

SNAKE PARENTHOOD

After mating, female snakes produce between 3 and 16 eggs or young, although some have as many as 100. Development time depends upon species and temperatures but as a rule snake eggs take 2–4 months to hatch. Eggs are laid below the surface of the soil or sand and are hatched by the sun. A young snake escapes from the egg by slashing through the shell using an egg tooth on its snout. If it is warm embryos develop faster, so some snakes are more choosy in where they lay their clutch. Piles of manure or rotting vegetation generate heat when they decay and these are prime "hot spots" for the eggs of grass snakes and some rat snakes. Termite

Green Tree Python. Coils perfectly along a branch while waiting to ambush its prey.

mounds with their toughened walls of mud and insect saliva are both safe and warm, maintained at a constant high temperature because of the heat produced by the millions of termites; where these occur many snakes exploit them as a natural incubator. Few snakes guard their eggs, but there are exceptions. Many pythons become "broody", coiling around their clutch in a protective embrace until their young begin to hatch. To keep their eggs at a higher temperature than the surrounding air, some pythons even generate body heat by violently twitching their muscles.

The king cobra is the only snake that builds an elaborate nest. The female uses her snout to clear the nest site of stones or sharp twigs before using a coil to gather in leaves and grasses. Once she has collected enough nesting material she weaves in and out of the pile to form a more compact mound. She then lays her eggs in a roofed chamber on top, remaining on guard until the baby cobras hatch.

Other snakes are live bearers, retaining their eggs within their bodies, before giving birth to a litter of babies. Each youngster is individually wrapped in its own egg membrane, and must use a tiny egg tooth to cut an exit in this transparent capsule.

Mothercare is over once there are young snakes on the scene, and the snakelings disperse and must find food and survive on their own.

SNAKES AND MAN

Throughout history and all around the world people have been enthralled by snakes. In some cultures they are sacred

creatures, believed to bring fertility and to possess the secret of immortality. It is likely that snakes were attributed with these powers because of their phallic form and the fact that they seem to be reborn with brighter colours and a more velvety feel every time they shed their skins. Skin shedding or sloughing is, in fact, the method used by snakes to accommodate growth and to replace their outer covering when it becomes abraded and worn. This happens 4 to 6 times in a year.

In other human societies snakes are the ultimate evil, demons from the underworld that are dealers in death. This fearsome reputation arose from their unblinking gaze, their sinuous rapid movements and above all from the extraordinary properties of venom. Before death a victim's limbs

Snakes have been both revered and loathed by man throughout history.

could swell grotesquely and he or she could even sweat blood from the pores, effects that were real and not imagined. But there is nothing supernatural about snakes; they just have elegant solutions to life without limbs.

Left to themselves, snakes are incapable of malevolence towards human beings; they never intentionally attack a person unless they are threatened themselves, either by accident or design. Unseen snakes can be trodden upon accidentally or, if they are noticed in the open, provoked by people trying to kill or harass them. Many snake bites could be avoided by a few simple precautions. In "snake territory" you should not go barefoot and care should be taken when putting your hands near rocks, burrows or dense vegetation that could be a reptilian retreat. A snake seen away from cover should not be molested, but left to slip away to go about its business, a business that is of great benefit to man.

In Maharashtra state in India in the small village of Shirala the people know the value of snakes. Every year in July there is the Festival of Nagpanchmi. Dancers, brass bands and a procession of decorated carts wend their way through the narrow village streets. People jostle at every vantage point eager to pay their respects to a beautiful creature. On every cart there are earthenware pots containing Indian cobras. Gently and with great care, handlers take out the snakes and show them to the crowd. The villagers know that these cobras control rats and mice that would otherwise consume their crops and spread disease. The snakes riding the carts will be released back into the fields where they were captured. Some have been caught, taken

part in the procession and then been released unharmed every year for a decade. Cobras will only bite a person in self-defence and the people of Shirala regard them with caution and respect, not fear and hatred. Shouldn't all snakes be treated the same?

HOW TO USE THIS BOOK

The species in this book are arranged in groups; blind snakes and thread snakes; pythons and boas; typical snakes; front-fanged snakes; vipers.

KEY TO SYMBOLS

Interesting facts about each snake have been provided by means of at-a-glance symbols, for which there are four categories. They denote whether a snake is:

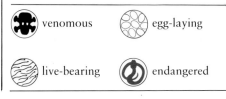

venomous   egg-laying

live-bearing   endangered

Trans-pecos Rat Snake. Primarily a nocturnal snake, feeding on birds, bats and lizards.

BLIND SNAKES (Family *Typhlopidae* and THREAD SNAKES (Family *Leptotyphlopidae*)

Considered to be primitive snakes, there are about 175 species of blind snakes and 80 species of thread snakes in the warmer parts of the world. Most of them are small, although some attain a length of 60cm (2ft). All are burrowers and look more like worms than snakes, with small overlapping scales, tiny heads and minuscule eyes.

BLIND SNAKE
Leptotyphlops humilis

Otherwise known as a worm snake due to its obvious resemblance to the common earthworm.
DESCRIPTION Up to 41cm (16in), but usually smaller. The vestigial eyes appear as dark spots under the scales of the blunt head. A shiny snake, the colour is purplish, brown or pink with a creamy underside.
DISTRIBUTION USA, southern California through to western Texas and into northwestern Mexico.
HABITAT Mostly found in arid areas but where there is some moisture in soil that is loose enough to burrow in. Occasionally found on the surface at night, but mostly dug out from under rocks, the roots of shrubs and around ant nests.
FOOD Feeds on small insects, especially ants, plus spiders, millipedes and centipedes.
BREEDING Lays a clutch of 2–6 tiny eggs.

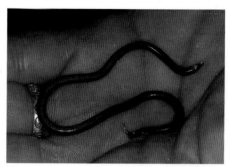

FLOWERPOT SNAKE
Rhamphotyphlops braminus

A tiny snake, named after its habit of hiding in the soil in flowerpots and the like.
DESCRIPTION A large specimen would be 15cm (6in) in length. These animals are black or chocolate with shiny scales, as if they have been polished. Tail ends in a spine.
DISTRIBUTION South East Asia, New Guinea and Northern Australia. Expanded its range by being accidentally introduced by man in containers of soil.
HABITAT Found in soil or under stones or logs, sometimes emerging at night through cracks in the floors of houses.
FOOD Worms, insects and their larvae.
BREEDING The only snake in the world to reproduce by virgin birth or parthenogenesis. All individuals are female and the eggs develop without fertilization.

PYTHONS (Family *Pythonidae* and BOAS (Family *Boidae*)

Includes all of the giant snakes. There are 37 species of boa and 27 species of python. They have vestiges of hind limbs that are seen as spurs at the base of the tail. They are primarily a tropical group although some small boas are found in more temperate climates. All subdue their prey by constriction. Pythons lay eggs; boas are live bearers. Many boas have a line of heat-sensitive pits along their lips so they can sense the body heat generated by their prey, even in pitch darkness.

BOA CONSTRICTOR
Boa constrictor

The classic constrictor often portrayed as a predator of man, yet these snakes are mainly placid and never grow big enough to consume a person.

DESCRIPTION To about 6 metres (20ft). A grey or silver snake with brown or deep red saddles along the back, though patterns and colour tend to be geographically variable.

DISTRIBUTION Central Mexico, Central and South America down to Argentina.

HABITAT From semi-arid regions to, more commonly, rain forest habitat. Mainly lives in the tree tops, only coming to the ground to forage, occasionally attracted to human habitations by the availability of rodents.

FOOD A constrictor, can manage quite large mammals and birds.

BREEDING Live-bearing; 20–50 young measuring 30cm (12in) in a litter.

DUMMERIL'S BOA
Acrantophis dumerili

Like most of Madagascar's wildlife, this snake is highly endangered.

DESCRIPTION Up to about 2 metres (6 ft). Ground colour a brownish-grey, with a richer red-brown on the back. The markings are deep

brown, a thin line across the back widening into a fairly regular double-lobed mark with a white centre to the lower part.

DISTRIBUTION Madagascar and the Mascarene Islands.

HABITAT Humid rain forests, sheltering in leaf litter, logs and mammal burrows. Hibernates during the dry, cool months from May to July

and breeds immediately upon emergence.
FOOD A constrictor, feeding on small mammals
and birds.
BREEDING Live-bearing; 4–6 large young are
produced.

ANACONDA
Eunectes murinus

The heaviest snake in the world, can grow to a
massive 130kgs (286lb). The source of many
myths, lengths of in excess of 18 metres (60ft)
have been claimed but a prize offered by the
New York Zoological Society for a 9 metres
(30ft) specimen remains unclaimed.
DESCRIPTION It is speculated that this species
can grow to more than 9 metres. Very heavy-
bodied brownish-green to greyish-green snake,
with ovoid markings in brown or black.
DISTRIBUTION Much of northern South America
and Trinidad.

HABITAT Semi-aquatic; restricted to swamps,
marshes and river valleys.
FOOD A constrictor capable of subduing and
consuming prey the size of young tapirs. Often
uses water to conceal itself from prey that
includes mammals, aquatic birds, caymans and
crocodiles.
BREEDING Live-bearing; between 10 and 50
young normally.

EMERALD TREE BOA
Corallus caninus

This snake gives an excellent example of convergent evolution as it is strikingly similar to the Australian green tree python, a snake that evolved in isolation thousands of miles away from this boa.

DESCRIPTION Bright green with a white or yellow belly and the back intermittently broken by bands and flecks of white. The young are similarly patterned, but a striking reddish-orange or bluish-green.

DISTRIBUTION The Amazon basin, Peru and Ecuador through Brazil and Bolivia to the Guianas.

HABITAT Totally arboreal, this snake uses its prehensile tail to grip branches while hanging loops of its body over the branches to be perfectly camouflaged during the day. Active at night, the adults forage high in the trees while the juveniles inhabit lower trees and bushes.

FOOD A constrictor, feeding on birds and mammals ambushed in the trees.

BREEDING Live-bearing, the young quickly making their way to lower parts of the trees.

RAINBOW BOA
Epicrates cenchria cenchria

Perhaps the most beautiful snake in the world, not just because of its markings but mainly due to the remarkable iridescence of the skin.
DESCRIPTION A medium-sized boa growing to a maximum of just over 2 metres (6ft). The skin is reddish brown with darker lateral rings and spots, but with microscopic ridges on the scales that act like a prism to refract light.
DISTRIBUTION Through much of northern South

America and into the Amazon Basin. Other rainbow boa sub-species range over most of South America.
HABITAT Found in forests, woodland and plains.
FOOD A constrictor, feeding on small mammals and birds.
BREEDING Live-bearing, producing litters of around 20 young.

PACIFIC ISLAND BOA
Candoia aspera

There are three species of Pacific Island boas; this is the smallest and plumpest.
DESCRIPTION Up to 1 metre (3ft) in length. Triangular head with a characteristic straight-edged snout. Its keeled scales have a row of diamond shaped markings.
DISTRIBUTION New Guinea, Moluccas, Bismarck Archipelego, Solomon and Tokelau Islands.

HABITAT Spends time in the trees and is fond of bathing.
FOOD Lives on a diet of small mammals, birds and lizards.
BREEDING Gives birth to a litter of living young.

ROSY BOA
Lichanura trivirgata

A normally tame snake but its nocturnal habits were alarming enough to the settlers of the western states of North America that they inevitably led to many snakes suffering a terminal fate at the hands of a "six-shooter".
DESCRIPTION A heavy-bodied snake up to 110cm (44in). Beige or rosy above, with blotched creamy underparts, prominent anal spurs and with a small elliptically pupilled iris.
DISTRIBUTION Southern parts of California and Arizona, Baja California and northwestern Mexico.
HABITAT Mostly nocturnal, living in arid areas, but sometimes found near water sources. When molested coils into a ball and protects the head with its body coils.
FOOD A constrictor, eating small mammals and birds.

BREEDING Live-bearing; clutches of between 3 and 12 young born in October or November.

RUBBER BOA
Charina bottae

A disturbed boa may curl into such a tight, spherical ball that it will roll with surprising ease.
DESCRIPTION 35–83cm (14–33in) long. A stout-bodied snake, with an extremely short and blunt tail. Its skin has a rubbery feel. The top of the head has large symmetrical scales; pupils vertically oval. It is plain brown to olive green above, yellow to cream below, usually with no pattern.
DISTRIBUTION Western North America. Mid

California to southern British Colombia, Pacific coast to central Wyoming. Wide altitude range, from sea-level up to 3,000m.
HABITAT A burrower found in grassland and woodland, especially below rotting logs and rocks.
FOOD Constrictor, eating young mice, shrews, salamanders and snakes.
BREEDING Live-bearing; 2–8 young born in later summer or early fall.

KENYAN SAND BOA
Eryx colubrinus loveridgii

An inoffensive snake, yet one that can suddenly and violently ambush prey, bursting out from beneath the sand to overpower the prey animal.
DESCRIPTION Up to about 95cm (38in). Usually a dark sandy-brown, with irregular blotches of dark brown on the back. occasionally black and silver individuals are found. The tail is very short and the head is small, with little in the way of a neck obvious.
DISTRIBUTION Ranges through much of east Africa.

HABITAT Found in dry bush and semi desert. A strong burrower, rarely seen at the surface except when dug up in such as maize fields (inevitably these individuals are accidentally killed during the process).
FOOD A constrictor, eating lizards and small rodents.
BREEDING Live-bearing, giving birth to around 20 young.

CALABAR GROUND PYTHON
Calabaria reinhardtii

Local people know this creature as the snake with two heads because when it moves above ground it waves its tail in the air, presumably to distract predators from attacking its head.
DESCRIPTION Up to 1 metre (3ft) in length. Its small head is not distinct from its cylindrical body. Brown to reddish brown, with reddish spots.
DISTRIBUTION West and central Africa.
HABITAT Like the sand boas this python is designed for burrowing, with a blunt head and smooth scales. It remains hidden in the day, amongst roots or in rotting logs, emerging at dusk to hunt. Curls into a ball when attacked. Inhabits rain forests and savannah.
FOOD Lizards and rodents.
BREEDING Little known. This snake is an egg layer, the number in each clutch being small.

BURMESE PYTHON
Python molorus

Snake dancers prefer this python above all others for their stage shows.

DESCRIPTION Reaches 8 metres (26ft) in length. Markings are an intricate pattern of irregular brown blotches on a yellow background.

DISTRIBUTION Southern Asia. Pakistan in the west to southern China in the east, and south to the Malay Archipelago.

HABITAT Often found near water, this sluggish python waits patiently for prey either coiled on the ground or hanging below a branch. In the cooler parts of its range it becomes torpid during the winter. Bharatpur Reserve in India is famous for its "hibernating" pythons.

FOOD Subdues mammals and birds by constriction. There is even a record of a 6 metre (20ft) python killing and eating a leopard.

BREEDING Lays as many as 100 eggs. The female coils around them until they hatch, twitching her muscles to generate heat if the air temperature becomes too cool.

ROYAL PYTHON
Python regius

Otherwise known as the "ball" python from its habit of rolling up into a tight ball when alarmed.

DESCRIPTION Usually no more than 1.5 metres (5ft). Smallest of the African pythons, it is stocky with a short tail. The ground colour is brown or bluish-brown, with a pattern of ovoid blotches of variable colour that normally includes yellow.

DISTRIBUTION West Africa, Sierra Leone, Togo, Senegal and Gambia.

HABITAT Forests and woodland, remaining dormant during the dry season, often holed up in tree crevices. Collected extensively for the pet and skin trades, these pythons are now considered threatened.

FOOD A constrictor, these snakes feed on small rodents and birds.

BREEDING Small clutches of between 2 and 7 eggs which the female broods under her coils for the 3 month incubation period.

RETICULATED PYTHON
Python reticulatus

The longest snake ever recorded, with one specimen found in Celebes in 1912 measuring 32ft 9½in (almost exactly 10 metres).
DESCRIPTION Up to about 10 metres (33ft), but relatively slim compared to its length. The striking colours and patterns allow the snake to blend into its surroundings.
DISTRIBUTION South East Asia, the Malay peninsula, Borneo, Java, Sumatra, Timor, Ceram and the Philippines.
HABITAT Rain forest and woodland, but most usually associated with rivers, lakes and their environs. A good swimmer, a fact that is reputed to account for its occurrence on many isolated islands.
FOOD A constrictor, feeding mostly on mammals and birds but also large lizards, like monitors, and snakes. There have also been rare reports of these snakes preying upon human beings.
BREEDING Lays eggs. As in most snakes, the size of the clutch will depend almost entirely on the size of the female.

BLACK-HEADED PYTHON
Aspidites melanocephalus

In cool weather this python will stick out its head from shelter so that the black scales absorb the heat of the sun.

DESCRIPTION Attains 2 metres (6ft) or more. Its head is jet black, while its body is yellowish or reddish brown with dark brown or black cross bands.

DISTRIBUTION Northern half of Australia.

HABITAT Found in humid coastal forests, dryish woodlands and grasslands. By day these pythons hide in burrows, hollow logs among tree roots, or in cavities in termite mounds. At night they hunt by probing into the retreats of their prey.

FOOD Ground-nesting birds, small mammals and reptiles including venomous snakes.

BREEDING Males indulge in ritualized combat during the breeding season. Female lays 5–12 eggs which she embraces with her body to guard until hatching.

BISMARCK RINGED PYTHON
Liasis boa

A relatively little-known snake, named for its geographical location rather than any relationship with the German statesman of the late nineteenth century.

DESCRIPTION Under 2 metres (6ft). The adults are poorly marked with black rings or are uniformly blackish-brown, usually with a light mark behind the eye. The juveniles are by far the more spectacular, being ringed in orange and black, a coloration that fades as the snake matures.

DISTRIBUTION The Bismarck Archipelago, Papua New Guinea.

HABITAT Found in rain forests, foraging actively for prey at night.

FOOD Constrictor, preying mainly on small rodents.

BREEDING Around a dozen eggs are brooded by the female.

CARPET PYTHON
Morelia spilotes variegata

Australia's best-known python, with a variety of distinctive subspecies. Can reach a length of 4 metres (13ft), although 2.5m (8ft) is the average.

DESCRIPTION All of the forms have a dark ground colour, blotched or patched with yellow or white markings which are bordered with black. The diamond python is the most distinctive and beautiful subspecies. The centre of each of the carpet python's dorsal scales is bright yellow or cream.

DISTRIBUTION Most of Australia except for the arid centre and the west.

HABITAT Equally at home on the ground or in the trees. Found in woodland, rocky outcrops and ravines, along water courses and in towns. Can even enter aviaries or chicken runs in search of food.

FOOD Small mammals and birds, although younger snakes prefer lizards.

BREEDING An average clutch contains 12–25 eggs. The female coils around them until they hatch, "shivering" her muscles to warm them if the temperature drops.

AMETHYSTINE PYTHON
Morelia amethistina

One of Australia's longest snakes, one specimen was measured and found to be 8.5 metres (28ft) long.

DESCRIPTION Usually grows up to 7 metres (23ft). A slender python with a prominent "neck". Olive brown in colour with bands of black that are usually broken up into irregular blotches.

DISTRIBUTION New Guinea and the northern part of Australia.

HABITAT Found in rain forests, savannah, woodland, even amongst scrubby vegetation on coral islets. At night these pythons either hang by their prehensile tails waiting to ambush prey or actively search for food in burrows, rock crevices or caves.

FOOD Rats, bandicoots, possums, fruit bats, wallabies and birds.

BREEDING The female lays 7–19 eggs which she coils herself around until they hatch about 3 months later.

GREEN TREE PYTHON
Chondropython viridis

Rests and waits for prey by folding its body along a branch in a series of perfectly measured loops, so that its head is always at the centre.

DESCRIPTION This snake can be 2 metres (6ft) long. Hatchlings are lemon yellow, getting the adult coloration at 1–3 years of age, which is an emerald green with the scales along the spine being white, yellow or cream.

DISTRIBUTION New Guinea and tip of north-eastern Australia.

HABITAT A denizen of humid rain forests, coiling in its characteristic fashion during the day and moving about at night.

FOOD Mammals, and especially birds, which it catches from ambush sites.

BREEDING 11–25 eggs that the female coils around, until hatching in about 50 days.

ROUGH SCALED PYTHON
Morelia carinata

Described by science in 1981, the first photographs of a living specimen were taken in 1992 by John Weigal of the Australian Reptile Park after an adventurous quest into unmapped territory.
DESCRIPTION Grows to 2 metres (6ft) in length. It is brown in colour and is unique amongst pythons in having keeled scales.
DISTRIBUTION Northern Kimberley District of Western Australia.
HABITAT Only a handful have been found in rainforest gorges, some amongst rocks, others in the trees.
FOOD Probably feeds on small mammals and birds.
BREEDING Unknown.

WATER PYTHON
Liasis fuscus

This snake can be so abundant there may be up to a tonne of pythons in a square kilometre.
DESCRIPTION Usually 1.5 metres (5ft) long, although some individuals are 3 metres (10ft). Blackish brown in colour, with a shiny appearance and fantastic iridescent scales.
DISTRIBUTION Northern Australia, New Guinea and the Lesser Sunda Islands.
HABITAT Found near rivers, swamps and billabongs. In the warmer part of the year spends most of its time in the water.

FOOD Small mammals including wallabies and water birds. Where it is extremely abundant the huge population is sustained primarily by dusky rats.
BREEDING Lays about a dozen eggs which the female coils around until hatching, shivering to warm them, if temperatures drop too low.

TYPICAL SNAKES (Family *Colubridae*)

Typical snakes contains about three quarters of all types of snakes, over 15,000 species. More detailed taxonomic studies are beginning to subdivide this "rag bag" group; for example, many authorities split off file snakes into a separate family. Most Colubrids are totally harmless to people, although some are not. The Twig snake (*Thelotornis kirtlandii*) and Boomslang (*Dispholidus typus*) have fangs at the back of their jaws and a potent venom.

CORN SNAKE
Elaphe guttata

Possibly the most popular captive snake, with a remarkable number of strains bred to enhance the differing colorations.

DESCRIPTION 60–180cm (2–6ft), a slender snake with a wide variety of colours but mainly from orange to grey with strong brown to red markings. First blotch on neck divides into two branches that extend forward to produce a spearpoint ending between the eyes. Usually exhibits a diagonal eyestripe and a chequerboard patterning against cream on the underside.

DISTRIBUTION Widely distributed throughout the southern and eastern USA and northeastern Mexico, with a few isolated populations outside that range.

HABITAT A strong climber, but mainly terrestrial. Occasionally found on farmland but more usually in woodland and on rocky slopes. Can be difficult to locate due to its propensity for hunting and resting underground in rodent burrows.

FOOD A constrictor, it eats small mammals, birds, lizards and frogs.

BREEDING Lays a clutch of 3–21 eggs from May to July.

GREEN RAT SNAKE
Elaphe triapsis

Elusive and poorly known but can be identified, even in poor light, by the fact that its head is longer than other American rat snakes.

DESCRIPTION 60–125cm (2–4ft). Slimly built, green or olive with no markings above and cream or whitish underparts. The scales are mostly weakly keeled, while the anal scale is divided.

DISTRIBUTION America, extreme south of Arizona and New Mexico through Mexico and into Guatemala and Costa Rica.

HABITAT Crepuscular and partially arboreal, it retires into rock crevices and underground at night.

FOOD A constrictor seeking out birds and their nestlings, but taking other prey, including small rodents and lizards.

BREEDING A clutch of in excess of 6 eggs is laid under stones or in similar locations.

BLACK RAT SNAKE
Elaphe obsoleta obsoleta

Otherwise known as the pilot snake, since it is believed to direct rattlesnakes and copperheads to hibernation sites.
DESCRIPTION A shiny black snake between 106cm (3½ft) and an exceptional 256cm (8½ft). Body shape in cross section is rectangular rather than round.
DISTRIBUTION Central and eastern USA, as far north as New York and Ontario, down to Louisiana and Oklahoma.
HABITAT A strong climber that may take up residence in tree cavities. Large numbers may congregate at traditional hibernation sites, often in the company of rattlesnakes or copperheads.
FOOD A constrictor, feeding on birds, small rodents and eggs.
BREEDING Lays up to 36 eggs in decomposing plant material.

TEXAS RAT SNAKE
Elaphe obsoleta lindheimeri

Known as the "meanest" American rat snake, this snake is often so aggressive that it never calms down, even after many years of captivity.
DESCRIPTION 106–218cm (3½–7ft). The brownish or bluish-black blotches are not heavily contrasted with the grey or yellowish ground colour. The head is often black, and red can be found on the skin between scales. There is a fair amount of variation in this species; however, the scales are keeled in all forms and the anal scale is divided.
DISTRIBUTION From the Mississippi Basin, west through Louisiana into central and southern Texas.
HABITAT USA, from swamps through to drier, rocky lands in the west of its range. Often found dead on the side of highways due to its habit of basking on the road surface.
FOOD A constrictor, feeding on small rodents, birds and eggs.
BREEDING The clutch of 6–28 eggs is laid from June to August.

GREY RAT SNAKE
Elaphe obsoleta spiloides

This snake is often associated with oak woodlands, from where it gets its alternative name, the "oak" snake.
DESCRIPTION 106–214cm (3½–7ft). This species is strongly blotched with, unlike most other rat snakes, similar markings to those of the juvenile. Blotches may be brown or grey, with a ground colour varying between grey, pale brown or nearly white. Scales are weakly keeled and the anal scale is divided.
DISTRIBUTION USA, from Georgia to Mississippi and in a band northwards to southern Indiana and Illinois.

HABITAT Found in farmland, on rocky slopes and in woodland. Where the species overlap it has a tendency to hybridize (or intergrade) with the black rat snake.
FOOD A constrictor, eating mainly small mammals, but it is also a favoured food of many hawks.
BREEDING Clutches of less than 30 smooth-shelled eggs are common.

TRANS-PECOS RAT SNAKE
Elaphe subocularis

Easily recognized, since it is the most "bug-eyed" snake within its range.
DESCRIPTION 86–168cm (3–5½ft), a yellowish olive to tan snake, with diagnostic dark H markings along the back. The head is broad for a rat snake and the eyes are particularly large and protrusive with an extra layer of small scales beneath them.
DISTRIBUTION Southern New Mexico through western Texas down to northern Central Mexico, mostly associated with the Chihuahuan Desert.
HABITAT Primarily nocturnal in arid or semi-arid locations, especially in rocky areas at an altitude of between 500–1,500 metres (1,500–5,000ft).
FOOD A constrictor feeding on rodents, bats, birds and lizards.
BREEDING Lays a clutch of 3–7 soft, leathery eggs in summer.

LADDER SNAKE
Elaphe scalaris

This snake's name refers to the H shape markings that run along the back of juveniles but normally fade by the time the snake is adult.
DESCRIPTION Up to 160cm (5ft) but normally less than 120cm (4ft). Large with smooth scales, an overhanging snout and a short tail. Adults are yellow-grey to brown, with a pair of dark brown stripes on the back; the belly is whitish or yellow but variably marked with black.
DISTRIBUTION Southwest Europe, most of Iberia, the Mediterranean coast of France and Minorca.
HABITAT Mostly diurnal, preferring stony habitats it can be often found in vineyards or around dry-stone walls. It can climb well and tends to be very aggressive if captured.
FOOD Constricts large prey, like a small rabbit, but eats variously sized mammals, nestling birds and grasshoppers, when young.
BREEDING Lays 6–12 eggs of about 5cm (2in) in length, in and around July.

LADDER SNAKE

FOUR-LINED SNAKE
Elaphe quatuorlineata

This is the longest snake in Europe, but its name can give the wrong impression as only the hatchlings and juveniles exhibit the four-lined pattern.

DESCRIPTION Up to 250cm (8ft), but generally under 150cm (5ft). Large with a long, slightly pointed, head and keeled scales that lend it a rather rough appearance. The most robust snake in its geographic region, it can also be distinguished by the presence of two preocular scales (directly in front of the eyes). Colour and pattern vary greatly, and the 4-lined markings fade as the snake gets older, but the belly is mainly an olivish yellow.

DISTRIBUTION Southeastern Europe into Russia, Italy, Sicily, many of the Aegean islands and South West Asia.

HABITAT Prefers humid areas near water, climbing and swimming well, often in overcast conditions or at dusk.

FOOD Constrictor, feeding on mammals, birds, eggs and lizards.

BREEDING May lay a clutch of around 20 eggs.

FOX SNAKE
Elaphe vulpina

The name fox snake originates from the fox-like odour that is associated with the fluid it discharges when threatened.

DESCRIPTION 91–179cm (3–6ft) long. Heavily blotched on the body and with a ground colour of yellowish to light brown; sometimes the head may be red-orange which can lead to its mis-identification as a copperhead.

DISTRIBUTION America, from southern Ontario south, between Indiana and Nebraska.

HABITAT Found in marshland, grass prairie, farmland and in riverine woodland. This snake is abundant in the marshy areas and dunes of the Great Lakes region and large numbers may congregate at hibernation sites.

FOOD A constrictor, feeds on rodents, frogs, birds and their eggs.

BREEDING 6–29 leathery eggs are deposited from late June to early August.

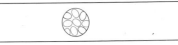

TAIWANESE BEAUTY SNAKE
Elaphe taeniurus

A common food item in the markets of Southern Asia, the Chinese also eat its gall bladder for reputed health-giving properties.
DESCRIPTION Up to 2 metres (6ft) long, it has a dark stripe from its eye to the back of its head. The body is black or grey with a scatter of dark blotches and a yellowish stripe along the back.
DISTRIBUTION Found over much of East and South East Asia.

HABITAT An adaptable snake of farmland, woods, villages and fields. An aggressive snake when approached in the wild.
FOOD Primarily rodents.
BREEDING 6–10 eggs laid in damp soil or rotting wood.

BULLSNAKE
Pituophis melanoleucus sayi

The name comes from the standard response to any threat, which includes an elevated head stance and sounds that have something in common with the snorts and grunts of a bull.
DESCRIPTION A large, 95–255cm (3–8½ft) long, yellowish snake with black, brown or reddish-brown blotches that are heaviest in contrast at the head and at the tail. The scales are keeled, while the belly is yellow with black spots and, unlike the rat snakes, it has a single anal scale.
DISTRIBUTION Found in a band through central USA, most northerly in Alberta and most southerly in eastern Mexico.
HABITAT A snake of the prairies and plains but ranges into the desert. When alarmed bullsnakes hiss loudly.
FOOD Constrictor, eating rodents, birds and eggs.

BREEDING Lays a clutch of up to 24 eggs in sandy soil or below large logs and rocks.

KANSAS GLOSSY SNAKE
Arizona elegans arenicola

There are records of this snake being killed by its food; glossy snakes have been found dead, pierced by the protruding scales of a horned lizard.
DESCRIPTION Up to 140cm (4½ft), a shiny cream snake with more than 50 separate brown body blotches. The scales are smooth, the belly is pale and unmarked, and the pupil of the eye is slightly elliptical.
DISTRIBUTION Nebraska and Kansas through West Texas and into Mexico.
HABITAT Nocturnal or crepuscular burrowers in mostly sandy areas. When alarmed the tail is vibrated to deter predators.
FOOD Constrictor, feeding on small rodents and lizards.
BREEDING Up to 24 eggs, the hatchlings are little carbon-copies of the adults.

SINALOAN MILK SNAKE
Lampropeltis triangulum sinaloae

The name milk snake came from the belief that they sucked the milk from the udders of cows. One of the 25 subspecies of the milk snake, this snake was only described by scientists in 1978. **DESCRIPTION** 102–122cm (3½–4ft). Head black,with some mottling of white, usually around the snout. The first black ring usually touches the angle of the jaw and creates a V shape on the throat; the red scales are not tipped black while the white scales are. There are between 10 and 16 red rings that are about three times the width of the black-white-black rings. All the body rings completely encircle the snake.
DISTRIBUTION Throughout Sinaloa, extending into neighbouring Mexican states.
HABITAT Little is known yet of this snake's natural history other than that it is found below 1,000 metres (3,000ft) and often around cornfields.

FOOD Small rodents, lizards and perhaps some invertebrates.
BREEDING Clutches are usually small, between 2 and 16.

HONDURAN MILK SNAKE
Lampropeltis triangulum hondurensis

It is thought by many that the striking "tri-colour" markings of milk snakes evolved originally as a form of mimicry of the highly venomous coral snake.
DESCRIPTION Up to 120cm (4ft). The head is black but with a distinct yellowish band on the snout and a second band that broadens as it makes its way from the top of the head. It has red-orange scales that may or may not be tipped with black. The body rings of red, black and yellow entirely encircle the body: there are 13–26 red body rings. Some specimens may lack yellow rings and have a generally dark or tangerine appearance.

DISTRIBUTION Much of Honduras, Nicaragua and possibly northeastern Costa Rica.
HABITAT Found at lower elevations, usually located under rotting logs or stumps, it is most active at night.
FOOD Able to subdue and eat a variety of other snakes, it also feeds on small lizards, mammals and birds.
BREEDING As with other milk snakes the eggs are remarkably long and cylindrical; deposited in rotting substrate, they hatch out around August.

PUEBLAN MILK SNAKE
Lampropeltis triangulum campbelli

Alongside Dixon's milk snake, this is the most recently discovered milk snake (1983).
DESCRIPTION 71–91cm (2–3ft). A distinctive snake, with broad white body bands and a white mottled snout. The tail has around 5 black and white bands with no red-orange bands; the average body rings are 16 white and red bands and 32 black. About half the red bands are not complete on the underside, while there is no black tipping of the white scales.

DISTRIBUTION Restricted to a small area of southern Mexico.
HABITAT Prefers arid areas at reasonable elevation, from 1,500 metres (5,000ft).
FOOD Small rodents, snakes and lizards are the most common prey items.
BREEDING Rarely deposits more than 14 elongated eggs, which have an incubation period of 6–9 weeks.

SCARLET KING SNAKE
Lampropeltis triangulum elapsoides

If you can remember the old rhyme, "Red and yellow kill a fellow . . ." then you can be sure that the snake you are identifying is or is not the highly venomous coral snake but the harmless scarlet king snake.
DESCRIPTION Up to 68cm (2¼ft). A mimic of the eastern coral snake, but the tip of the snout is red and the yellow rings are separated from the red by black. The yellow bands may sometimes be white; all bands generally continue across the belly.
DISTRIBUTION North America, from southeastern Virginia through much of the eastern USA down to the tip of Florida, west to the Mississippi.
HABITAT Especially fond of pine woodland, hiding behind bark or underneath logs and often wintering in tree stumps.
FOOD A constrictor, feeds on lizards, snakes, baby rodents, fish, insects and earthworms.
BREEDING 2–15 eggs are laid in June or July.

GREY-BANDED KING SNAKE
Lampropeltis alterna

Was once considered to be a rare snake, but is actually quite common, its nocturnal habits accounted for the fact that it was rarely seen. **DESCRIPTION** Up to 150cm (5ft). Has quite a distinct head shape, grey with black lines or dots. Its pattern consists of a series of white-edged, red-centred, black blotches, the rest of the body being grey. There are between 9 and 39 black blotches or saddles, giving an indication of how variable a snake this can be. A distinctive characteristic is the relatively large eye with its silvery-grey iris.

DISTRIBUTION Southern Texas and into northern Mexico.
HABITAT Partial to arid to semi-humid habitats ranging from desert through to mountains. Nocturnal and secretive, once believed rare but now known to be abundant, it is able to pass an evil-smelling musk when captured.
FOOD Almost exclusively feeds on lizards, but will occasionally take small rodents.
BREEDING Small clutches of eggs are generally deposited beneath stones. •

CALIFORNIA KING SNAKE
Lampropeltis getulus californiae

Like many of the king snakes, this snake is relatively immune to the venom of rattlesnakes.
DESCRIPTION The ground colour for this snake is brown or black with stripes or rings of white or cream. The ringed form is the most common throughout its range.
DISTRIBUTION Ranges down the west coast of America from Oregon down through Baja California, and its eastward boundaries run from Nevada down into Mexico.

HABITAT A wide range of habitats, from rivers and grassland to desert or forest. Mostly diurnal, but more crepuscular in arid areas.
FOOD A constrictor, eating eggs, lizards, birds, amphibians, rodents and snakes, including rattlesnakes.
BREEDING 6–24 eggs in a clutch that may be deposited in rotting logs.

FLORIDA KING SNAKE
Lampropeltis getulus floridana

A snake that counts the highly venomous copperhead and coral snakes as choice prey items.
DESCRIPTION 90–176cm (3–6ft). A beautifully marked snake, with most scales brown edged with cream, and usually with small light bands present across the back.
DISTRIBUTION Primarily found in southern Florida, but intergrades with the eastern king snake in much of the rest of Florida.
HABITAT Mostly diurnal, but may forage more actively at dawn and dusk; usually in wetter areas, but may be found in a wide variety of habitats.
FOOD A constrictor, readily taking any snake of a similar size or smaller than it, otherwise eats rodents and eggs.
BREEDING Up to and above 20 cylindrical eggs are laid in late May.

INDIGO SNAKE
Drymarchon corais

This is the largest North American snake; its old common names, like blue bullsnake, originated from its use in carnivals by snake charmers.
DESCRIPTION 150–250cm (5–8ft). A large, beautifully shiny, blue-black snake. Chin and sides of head may be slightly red or orange-brown, scales mostly smooth, with a single anal scale.
DISTRIBUTION Divided into two subspecies. The eastern, primarily in the Florida panhandle, and the Texas, in arid southern Texas, into eastern Mexico.
HABITAT Defends itself by flattening its neck vertically, hissing and rattling its tail, though it rarely bites if caught. Often to be found in the burrows of the gopher tortoise.
FOOD Not a constrictor, its varied diet includes small mammals, birds, frogs and snakes, most impressively venomous species like cottonmouths and rattlesnakes.
BREEDING Lays 5–12 leathery eggs; hatchlings emerge from late July through to October.

RACER
Coluber constrictor

Named for its ability to disappear into undergrowth at, apparently, fantastic speeds.
DESCRIPTION 50–180cm (1½–6ft). Has developed into a variety of subspecies and hybrids (or intergrades); exhibiting a range of coloration though this, the nominate species, is black. Generally the scales are smooth and the anal scale is divided, and specifically the lower preocular scale wedged between the upper labial scales. Broad headed, slim with large eyes, adults are usually plain-coloured above, while the young are blotched.
DISTRIBUTION Throughout USA except parts of the extreme north and southwestern central states.
HABITAT An extremely fast-moving snake, the racer is also partially arboreal. Diurnal, hunting with head characteristically held above the ground. Mainly absent from high altitudes and very dry locations.
FOOD Not a constrictor. Eats rodents, birds, lizards, snakes, frogs and insects.
BREEDING 2–31 eggs laid in June to August.

WESTERN WHIP SNAKE
Coluber viridiflavus

The snake most often encountered in Mediterranean holiday areas, although any sightings are likely to be very short as this snake "whips" into brush and out of view.

DESCRIPTION Maximum length 200cm (7½ft), but more normally 150cm (5ft). Heavily marked in irregular crossbars or totally black above, otherwise yellowish becoming paler on the belly with occasional black spotting. The upper markings become striped longitudinally towards the tail, while the fairly prominent eye has a round pupil.
DISTRIBUTION Northern Spain, much of France, Switzerland, Sardinia and Italy.
HABITAT Diurnal and largely terrestrial, a fast and agile snake locating prey by sight. Frequents a variety of mainly dry habitats below 1,500 metres (5,000ft).
FOOD Not a constrictor. Eats small rodents, nesting birds, snakes (including vipers), lizards, frogs and grasshoppers.
BREEDING 5–15 eggs laid in a clutch.

GREEN WATER SNAKE
Nerodia cyclopian

Easily mistaken for the highly venomous cottonmouth.

DESCRIPTION A heavy-bodied snake between 76–127cm (2½–4ft). Identification is difficult, few markings being distinguishable on the greenish or brownish back, but best recognized by a row of scales that are present between the eye and the lip scales.

DISTRIBUTION USA, primarily in the Mississippi Valley.

HABITAT A diurnal species, often found basking on low tree limbs near water. They can be found in great numbers in undisturbed areas, normally near quiet waters.

FOOD Primarily eating small fish such as minnows.

BREEDING Live-bearing; perhaps over 100 young produced in a litter.

SOUTHERN WATER SNAKE
Nerodia fasciata

Usually the most placid of the water snakes, often only regurgitating their last meal upon any assailant before making their escape.
DESCRIPTION 61–152cm (2–5ft). Can be identified by the dark stripe from the eye to the angle of the jaw, spots at the side of the belly and dark bands across the back. Colours usually darken with age, even to black, but can vary between grey, tan and red with red, brown or black bands.
DISTRIBUTION USA, in a coastal band from North Carolina to Alabama.
HABITAT Found in virtually every freshwater habitat from slow-moving streams through to marshes and even into saltwater regions.
FOOD Salamanders, frogs and small fish.
BREEDING Live-bearing; litters of up to 57 young are born from June to August.

GRASS SNAKE

GRASS SNAKE
Natrix natrix

There are some populations of black (melanistic) grass snakes and some individuals that play dead when attacked.

DESCRIPTION Normally up to 120cm (4ft) but sometimes as much as 200cm (6½ft). Most specimens have a characteristic collar of yellow or white; the body is olive-grey, greenish to even silvery-grey with dark blotches and stripes.

DISTRIBUTION Virtually all of Europe below the Arctic Circle, across into Russia and south into Iran and Iraq.

HABITAT Marshes, meadowlands, farmland and hillside adjacent to rivers. Famous for its habit of voiding the contents of its anal gland when handled and can even feign death when threatened.

FOOD Feeds mainly on frogs and toads, but also takes fish, tadpoles, newts and even small mammals.

BREEDING Females can retain their eggs for up to 2 months; shortening the incubation period has allowed this snake to extend its range north. Deposits its eggs in decomposing plant material; often more than one female will use a single nest site.

DICE SNAKE
Natrix tessellata

An extremely aquatic snake, spending more of its time in water than any other European water snake.

DESCRIPTION Up to around 100cm (3½ft). It has a rather small, pointed head, but can also be distinguished by the pattern of dark square markings that lend the snake its name. The ground colour can vary between greyish and brownish-green; some populations may be black or even yellow.

DISTRIBUTION Southeastern Europe to Afghanistan, Pakistan and even into China.

HABITAT Always found close to or in water. May climb small trees, but if disturbed will immediately drop into the water to escape.

FOOD Almost totally piscivorous but will take amphibians.

BREEDING Having mated after hibernation, the females lay up to 24 eggs under rotted logs or stones.

VIPERINE SNAKE
Natrix maura

This snake can be confused with a viper due to the presence of zigzag markings on the back, but if seen in water it will almost always be safe to assume it is the viperine snake.

DESCRIPTION Normally reaches around 70cm (2½ft) in length. Usually exhibits some dark markings on the small, but broad, head. Individuals are usually brown or grey with a pattern of dark markings down the back and dark blotches on the side, mainly with light centres.

DISTRIBUTION Southwestern Europe, Sardinia and parts of North Africa.

HABITAT Diurnal, chiefly found in or around water, preferring weedy ponds and rivers. Dives readily when disturbed; if cornered will strike repeatedly, but with its mouth closed.

FOOD Eats frogs, toads, newts, tadpoles, fish and even earthworms.

BREEDING 5–20 eggs are laid in June to July, and hidden under rocks, in sand or in decaying vegetation.

COMMON GARTER SNAKE
Thamnophis sirtalis

The most widely distributed snake in North America.

DESCRIPTION 46–124cm (1½–4ft) long. Characteristically has 3 yellowish lateral stripes and a double row of spots between the stripes that may actually predominate in some individuals. However, this snake is extremely variable; some specimens are virtually stripeless, black, green, brown and olive being among the ground colours individuals may exhibit. The scales are keeled and, like most garter snakes, it is distinguished from the water snakes by having a single anal scale.

DISTRIBUTION Southern Canada to the Gulf coast and west to California, only missing from the desert regions of southwest North America.
HABITAT A common snake found in woodland, marshes, along rivers and drainage ditches and even in city parks.
FOOD Mainly eats amphibians, tadpoles and earthworms.
BREEDING Live-bearing, producing 7–85 young between June and October.

RED-SIDED GARTER SNAKE
Thamnophis sirtalis parietalis

The famous inhabitant of Canada's snake dens.
In areas where hibernation sites are at a
premium, thousands of snakes gather at prime
sites.
DESCRIPTION Grows to about 60cm (2ft) long.
Black in colour with a strip of yellow along its
back and two yellow stripes on its side. It gets
its name from the red bars between the back
and side stripes.
DISTRIBUTION Much of Canada and the USA.
HABITAT In the northern part of its range
hibernates for much of the year. Sometimes
climbs low bushes to get to birds' nests.
FOOD Amphibians, worms, the odd rodent and
baby birds.
BREEDING In communal hibernation sites these
snakes can have an extraordinary mating
system. In spring mating balls are formed with
up to 30 males trying to mate with one female.
Some males exude the same pheromones from
their skins as females, so they distract the other
males in the ball and have a better chance to
mate. Live bearers, producing up to 15 young.

SMOOTH SNAKE
Coronella austriaca

The rarest snake in England, but common
throughout much of the rest of its range, even
taking up residence in gardens.
DESCRIPTION Usually up to 60cm (2ft). It has a
small head, small eyes with round pupils and a
cylindrical body. Usually grey but grading up to
reddish, with a slightly darker head, a strong
stripe from the neck through the eye and a
series of irregular small dark spots on the back.
DISTRIBUTION Much of western Europe except
southern Spain, much of Britain and northern
Scandinavia. To the east it continues into
Russia, Asia Minor and northern Iran.
HABITAT Diurnal, though secretive. Prefers dry
habitats like sandy heathland, bushy slopes and
embankments.
FOOD Relies heavily on a diet of lizards, though
will also take small snakes, mammals and
insects.
BREEDING Live-bearing; 2–15 young in a litter.

EGG EATING SNAKE
Dasypeltis scabra

Renowned for its ability to swallow eggs far greater in diameter than that of the snake itself.
DESCRIPTION Up to 105cm (3½ft). A thin snake with a surprisingly small head, considering its diet. Normally brownish, but occasionally grey or black, with a black "chain" of diamond-shaped markings along the back. The scales are heavily keeled on the back and serrated on the sides.
DISTRIBUTION North East Africa, southern Arabia, west to Gambia and down to South Africa.
HABITAT Partially arboreal, even using birds' nests it has just robbed as resting places. It is found in a variety of habitats apart from rain forest or desert. When molested this snake mimics the defensive actions of venomous snakes, either rasping its scales or puffing up, hissing and feigning aggressive strikes.
FOOD Solely feeds on eggs, using not teeth but projections from its vertebrae to break open the swallowed egg before regurgitating the drained shell.

BREEDING Up to 18 eggs in a clutch.

WESTERN HOGNOSE SNAKE
Heterodon nasicus

Famed for its defensive displays, which range from bluff through to full-scale death-feigning.
DESCRIPTION Up to 90cm (3ft). A heavy-bodied snake with thick neck and distinctively upturned nose. Colours range from cream to brown, with heavy light to dark brown blotching along the body and characteristic black markings on the underside of the tail.
DISTRIBUTION Southern Canada ranging south in a wide band through much of central USA and down into northern Mexico.
HABITAT Prefers open land, prairies, sparse woodland, farmland, floodplains and into semi-arid and canyon areas. Uses its broad snout to burrow and its enlarged back teeth in holding prey.
FOOD Mildly venomous. Toads are this snake's staple food, but it will also take frogs, salamanders, lizards, snakes and reptile eggs.
BREEDING A clutch of 4–23 eggs is laid.

EASTERN HOGNOSE SNAKE
Heterodon platyrhinos

Like the Western hognose this snake may provide clues as to how venom evolved; though it has enlarged rear teeth and a very mild venom, it has no real mechanism for introducing this venom to prey.
DESCRIPTION 51–115cm (1½–4ft). A stocky snake with a distinctly less upturned nose than its western counterpart. The ground colours are variable, ranging from yellow through grey, brown to even red; some individuals are plain black or grey, but spotted specimens are the norm.

DISTRIBUTION Much of eastern and central USA.
HABITAT Active during the day it spends most of its time foraging for prey, often burrowing into root systems to locate toads. Like the Western Hognose, it will feign death as well as inflate the neck and strike.
FOOD Mildly venomous. Toads form the majority of its diet, but frogs may also be eaten.
BREEDING Lays a clutch of 5–61 eggs.

SCARLET SNAKE
Cemophora coccinea

An impressive mimic of the eastern coral snake when seen at a distance, easier to identify if you can get a closer look.
DESCRIPTION 36–82cm (1¼–2½ft). Distinguished by having markings that form a saddle pattern rather than a banded pattern, a very pointed, red snout and a plain whitish belly.
DISTRIBUTION USA, in many of the eastern seaboard states north to New Jersey, down to Florida, through to Texas and north to Montana.
HABITAT Found in loose-soiled open woodland. A burrower rarely found at the surface, more normally disturbed under logs or by agricultural practices.
FOOD A constrictor, feeding on small mice, lizards and snakes, and proving very partial to snakes' eggs.
BREEDING Females lay 3–8 leathery and elongated eggs in a clutch.

SMOOTH GREEN SNAKE
Opheodrys vernalis

The green dorsal colour of this snake changes to a dull blue or grey after death.
DESCRIPTION 30–65cm (1–2ft). A slender plain green snake with a white or yellowish belly grading up to bright yellow under the tail.
DISTRIBUTION Occurs in much of northeastern USA and some parts of southern Canada as well as isolated populations in southern Texas and Idaho, New Mexico and Wyoming.
HABITAT Mostly terrestrial in grassy areas in forests, prairies and along river edges.
FOOD Eats mainly insects and spiders.
BREEDING Several females may share a nest site where each will lay a clutch of 3–18 eggs.

MANGROVE SNAKE
Boiga dendrophila

A spectacular animal that is a popular "draw" in snake charming shows.

DESCRIPTION Grows up to 2.5 metres (8ft). A glossy black snake with 40–50 sulphur yellow bars. The eye has vertical pupils like a cat's.

DISTRIBUTION Thailand and the Malay peninsular, Philippines and Indonesia.

HABITAT Mangroves and tropical rain forests, where it is often found in the trees.

FOOD Small mammals, birds, eggs and reptiles. Large fangs at the back of its mouth can deliver quite a potent venom.

BREEDING Lays a clutch of eggs in damp soil or rotting wood.

BOOMSLANG
Dispholidus typus

When angered, this snake inflates its throat to produce an alarming threat display to potential predators.

DESCRIPTION Averages 120–150cm (4–5ft). It possesses a very short head with large eyes and a slender body. The colour varies markedly, even within the same geographic location.

DISTRIBUTION Africa, south of the Sahara.

HABITAT Totally arboreal, the name boomslang comes directly from the Afrikaans meaning "tree snake".

FOOD One of the most notorious and venomous snakes in Africa, back-fanged but because of its short head the enlarged fangs are in fact relatively near the front of the mouth. It preys on chameleons, other lizards, amphibians and birds, often found raiding weaver bird colonies.

BREEDING Up to 24 eggs deposited that require about 6 months' incubation before the 30cm (1ft) hatchlings emerge.

GOLDEN FLYING SNAKE
Chrysopelea ornata

One of the 5 species of snakes that can spread their ribs and glide from tree to tree.
DESCRIPTION Grows to about 1.3 metres (4ft). An athletic, slender snake with large eyes. Its coloration is green with each scale bordered and bisected by black.
DISTRIBUTION India and Sri Lanka, Indonesia, southern China and the Malay peninsular.
HABITAT A denizen of tropical rain forests, it is

diurnal, arboreal and sun loving. Moves with alacrity in the tree tops by climbing, jumping and gliding. Back-fanged, but they have a weak venom.
FOOD Lizards and frogs. May take an hour or more to subdue a lizard.
BREEDING Comes down to the ground to lay eggs in leaf mould on the forest floor.

VINE SNAKE
Oxybelis aeneus

May attempt to mimic the branches they habitually lie along by appearing to sway in the breeze.
DESCRIPTION 90–150cm (3–5ft). An incredibly slender and long-headed snake, with comparatively small eyes and a long tail (up to half its body length). Generally greyish-brown above, grey below, with white or yellow under the head, an eye stripe and distinctive cream lips.
DISTRIBUTION Extreme South Arizona into Central and South America.
HABITAT Active during daylight hours, mainly arboreal, often being found along thin branches, in a range of arid to moist habitats. Bluffs when disturbed with a wide-gaping mouth.
FOOD Back-fanged and mildly toxic, feeds mainly on lizards.

BREEDING A clutch of 3–5 eggs is laid in spring and summer.

FRONT-FANGED SNAKES (Family *Elapidae*)

About 240 species, all with short, fixed fangs for injecting venom.
Found throughout the warmer parts of the world, but particularly in
Australia where 9 out of 10 species are elapids. Some authorities
consider that these, as well as the sea snakes should be classed in their
own families.

SEA KRAIT
Laticauda colubrina

Can be found in large numbers when they come
ashore to breed.
DESCRIPTION Up to 1.5 metres (5ft) in length.
Its coloration is bluish grey with cross bands of
black. They head is marked with black and
yellow.
DISTRIBUTION Tropical seas and shores from
India through Indonesia, Malaysia, New
Guinea, Australia and the Pacific Islands.
HABITAT Mainly aquatic, but also found on the
land in rocky and coral crevices. Venom is toxic
but this snake has a placid disposition and does
not bite even when freshly caught.
FOOD Forages at night, grabbing sleeping fish
from rock crevices.
BREEDING It comes ashore to lay eggs.

FIERCE SNAKE
Parademansia microlepidota

The land snake with the most potent venom. A
large one has the potential to dispatch 250,000
mice.
DESCRIPTION 2 metres (6½ft) is the average
length. Usually a brown snake, with some of its
scales edged with black or brown. Some
populations have a distinct black head.
DISTRIBUTION Australia in western Queensland,
northwestern South Australia and western New
South Wales.

HABITAT Found in stony deserts or dry flood
plains with deep cracking clays and soils.
Abroad in daylight, it often lives in the burrows
of its main prey, the plague rat.
FOOD Rodents.
BREEDING Lays a clutch of 9–12 eggs which
hatch in about 70 days.

FIERCE SNAKE

COLLETT'S SNAKE
Pseudechis colletti

Potentially fatal to people, this rare and beautiful Australian snake keeps itself to itself and there is no proof that it has ever bitten anyone.

DESCRIPTION Total length is about 2.5 metres (8ft). The snake has a brown or black body colour, with blotches of orange or red that merge together at the sides.

DISTRIBUTION Only found in central Queensland, Australia.

HABITAT Generally near rivers in black soil flood plains or riverine forests. It is so uncommon and elusive that little is known about its behaviour.

FOOD Small mammals, lizards, frogs and birds.

BREEDING Lays 7–14 eggs in October to December.

EASTERN TIGER SNAKE
Notechis scutatus

The venomous snake that is common in the most densely populated areas of Australia.
DESCRIPTION A bulky snake that can grow to nearly 2 metres (6½ft) in length. Very variable in colour, can be grey, green, brown or even black with a series of lighter cross bands.
DISTRIBUTION East and south eastern Australia.
HABITAT Usually found in damp habitats. Unaggressive, but holds its ground, so it can be trodden upon accidentally; before an anti-venom was developed it was responsible for human fatalities.
FOOD Specializes in frogs, but will take birds and rodents.
BREEDING Males indulge in "ritualized combats" during the spring. After mating the female retains her eggs within her body, eventually giving birth to 30 or so young.

BLACK TIGER SNAKE
Notechis ater

Some island populations of this snake fast for 10 months of the year.
DESCRIPTION There are a variety of subspecies that range in size from 1–2.4 metres (3–8ft). All are heavily built, with broad heads. The colour is dark brown or black, with some of the western populations having lighter bands.
DISTRIBUTION Western Australia, southern Australia, Tasmania and small islets and islands off Australia's southern coast.
HABITAT Found in marshlands, sand dunes or dry rocky deserts. Some of the island forms spend most of their time in sea bird burrows.
FOOD Frogs, birds and rodents. Two of the island subspecies survive by feeding upon mutton birds, a type of shearwater. The snakes must gorge on chicks when the shearwaters are breeding, then fast for 10 months, when the mutton birds are out at sea. Juvenile tiger snakes live on lizards until they are big enough to eat a bird.
BREEDING Females give birth to 6–20 young (sometimes more) in mid to late summer.

TAIPAN
Oxyuranus scutellatus

The largest and most notorious venomous snake in Australia, with the longest fangs (12mm [½in]) to boot.
DESCRIPTION Can grow to 3.5 metres (11½ft) but more usually 1.5 metres (5ft). It has large glittering eyes set in a creamy head, with a body of light to dark brown becoming lighter at the sides.
DISTRIBUTION North and northeastern Australia.
HABITAT Found in sugar cane fields, farms, rubbish dumps and woodlands. If given the chance a taipan will always retreat from people but if provoked will strike repeatedly.
FOOD A rodent specialist, which is why it is attracted to farms and dumps where there are large populations of mice.
BREEDING Lays 10–12 eggs.

DEATH ADDER
Acanthophis antarcticus

Perfectly camouflaged, it wiggles the tip of its tail to lure unwary prey.

DESCRIPTION Fat body, usually under 1 metre (3ft) in length. Very variable in colour; red, grey or brown with cross bands that can be either darker or lighter than the overall ground colour.

DISTRIBUTION The whole of Australia except the southeastern corner.

HABITAT Forests or scrubland with sand or leaf litter in which it can hide. A "sit and wait" predator that flicks its tail to lure inquisitive prey within striking distance.

FOOD Reptiles, small mammals and birds.

BREEDING A live-bearer that produces a litter of 15–20 babies.

KING BROWN SNAKE
Pseudechis australis

Under threat in the northern part of its range from the lethal effects of swallowing cane toads.

DESCRIPTION Up to 2 metres (6½ft) long. Each scale can be edged or tipped with black, resulting in a reticulated pattern on an all-ground colour of copper or brown.

DISTRIBUTION The whole of Australia, except the south and the east.

HABITAT Found in nearly every type of habitat from tropical forests to arid desert. In cool weather this snake is active during the day, becoming nocturnal in hotter seasons or climates.
FOOD Small mammals, birds and frogs. For the snake, cane toads seem a perfect food except that they are toxic and eating one causes death. Native animals have yet to come to terms with an introduced species.

BREEDING Ritualised combat has been observed between males during the breeding season (October and November). After mating the female lays about 10 eggs.

CORAL SNAKE
Micruroides euryxanthus

Despite possessing a potent venom, this snake generally defends itself with sound; waving its tail above its body and extruding its cloaca produces "popping" sounds.
DESCRIPTION No more than about 50cm (20in) long. The body is totally encircled by clearly defined glossy, black, yellow and red bands. The edges of the scales are tipped black, while the head is black from the snout to just behind the termination of the mouth.
DISTRIBUTION Northern Mexico into New Mexico and Arizona.

HABITAT Found in areas of sandy soil in rocky locations emerging from burrows or under rocks at night and during overcast conditions.
FOOD Venomous, feeding almost entirely on snakes, especially the blind snake, *Leptotyphlops*.
BREEDING 2–3 eggs laid under a rock or in a burrow.

EASTERN CORAL SNAKE
Micrurus fulvius

Highly venomous but inoffensive, will rarely bite except under extreme circumstances.
DESCRIPTION Up to around 90cm (3ft). The yellow bands are narrow and border the black and red bands; there is some flecking of black in the red bands. The black on the head reaches only to just beyond the eyes.
DISTRIBUTION Southeastern USA, and from southern Arkansas west into Texas and south into Mexico.

HABITAT A secretive snake, it often remains hidden in leaf debris or burrows, only emerging into its woodland or riverine habitat on humid or overcast days.
FOOD Venomous, feeding on small prey items, snakes, lizards and nestling rodents.
BREEDING Deposits up to 18 eggs in rotten logs or stumps.

BUSHMASTER
Lachesis muta

It is reputed that female bushmasters actively and aggressively guard their nest sites.

DESCRIPTION Normally 210–240cm (7–8ft), but sometimes up to 350cm (12ft). The ground colour can vary between yellowish, reddish and grey-brown, marked down the back by a series of dark brown blotches that stretch down the sides to form dark lateral triangles.

DISTRIBUTION Much of Central America and into Peru, the Guianas and into Brazil.

HABITAT Resides almost exclusively in primary and secondary forests and adjacent cleared areas. Mostly nocturnal, foraging for prey on the ground, in burrows and around exposed root systems.

FOOD Venomous, most normally feeding on small mammals, but occasionally eating birds and amphibians.

BREEDING Lays about 12 eggs in a clutch.

SOUTH AFRICAN SPITTING COBRA
Hemachatus hemachatus

"Rinkhals" is the Afrikaans name, referring to the distinctive white throat band.

DESCRIPTION A large stout cobra that is dingy black or brown. Averages about 1 metre (3ft) in length. The only cobra with keeled body scales.

DISTRIBUTION Zimbabwe and South Africa.

HABITAT Found in a variety of habitats where it hides in scrubby vegetation or rock piles. When defending itself it can spit venom for up to 3 metres (10ft).

FOOD Rodents and toads.

BREEDING A live-bearer, which is unusual for a cobra. It gives birth to a litter of 63 young in the autumn.

MOZAMBIQUE SPITTING COBRA
Naja mossambica

The "red spitter" can spray two jets of venom from tiny holes in the tips of its fangs for up to 2.5 metres (8ft).

DESCRIPTION Usually attaining a length of 1.5 metres (5ft) but on occasions reaching up to 2.8 metres (9ft). Its coloration ranges from brown-red, pinkish to orange-red; there are often black cross bands or blotches on the throat.

DISTRIBUTION Southern Tanzania, Mozambique, Botswana and northern South Africa.

HABITAT Ground dwelling, sheltering in termite mounds and rock crevices, it basks during the day and forages at night. Quick to rouse and to spit, it will also bite readily, though the venom rarely causes fatalities.

FOOD Venomous, eating toads, snakes, birds, rodents and even eggs.

BREEDING Between 10 and 22 eggs are laid in summer.

FOREST COBRA
Naja melanoleuca

Though a slender snake it is the largest of the African cobras.

DESCRIPTION Up to 2.5 metres (8ft). It appears black unless in good light, when a distinct pale flecking of the scales is obvious. The front of the snout, parts of the face and the underside are a bright orange-yellow; on the belly this is broken by a black band under the hood.

DISTRIBUTION Central Africa, south to Angola and eastern parts of South Africa.

HABITAT Occurs in heavily forested areas or along forest edges.

FOOD Venomous, small mammals.

BREEDING Lays 15–26 large eggs in leaf litter or hollow logs.

KING COBRA
Ophiophagus hannah

The largest venomous snake in the world with gigantic fangs long enough to penetrate the hide of an elephant and enough venom to kill it.

DESCRIPTION Usually 4 metres (13ft) in length, but the maximum ever recorded was over 5.5 metres (18ft). Medium to dark brown with dull light and dark cross bands along the body.

DISTRIBUTION India, Indo-China to southern India, and the Indo-Australia Archipelago.

HABITAT A denizen of tropical rain forests. For most of the year shy and wary of human beings, but females can become aggressive when guarding the nest. A king cobra rearing up over 1 metre (3ft) off the ground in a threat display can make for an exciting encounter.

FOOD Rodents and reptiles, with a predilection for other snakes.

BREEDING The only snake in the world that builds an elaborate nest. The female lays up to 40 eggs, staying on guard until they hatch.

MONOCLED COBRA
Naja naja

India's good snake, a valuable exterminator of rats and mice.

DESCRIPTION A large specimen would attain 2 metres (6½ft) in length. Typically yellowish or dark brown, with a black and white spectacle marking on the neck that is only obvious when the snake is aroused and the hood is spread. There is also a pair of black and white spots on the undersurface of the hood.

DISTRIBUTION Southern Asia and Indo-Australian archipelago.

HABITAT Found in a wide range of habitats; forest, farmland, even towns. Fast and agile it slips away at the footfall of people. Revered in the mythologies of India and Egypt.

FOOD Mice, frogs and reptiles.

BREEDING Lays 10–20 eggs.

BLACK MAMBA
Dendroaspis polylepis

With a top speed of 23kmh (14mph), this snake is reputedly the fastest in the world.

DESCRIPTION A very large snake up to 430cm (14ft) long. Seldom, if ever, black; they are generally olive-grey to mottled brown with a satiny sheen. The interior of the mouth is, in fact, the only part of the snake that is black. The head is slightly flattened at the sides, making it appear heavier than in many other species from side on.

DISTRIBUTION Africa, from southern Ethiopia down to the Cape.

HABITAT Diurnal and mostly terrestrial, but will climb to bask and search for prey. Said to be as fast and agile in branches or undergrowth as on open ground, it must forage extensively to support such vigorous activity. It has an incredibly high rate of digestion, helped by the potency of the venom, and can digest a large rat in under an hour.

FOOD Highly venomous, it kills prey with a neurotoxin that in human beings could cause death by asphyxia. Eats rodents (including squirrels), hyraxes, birds, bats and lizards.

BREEDING Lays a clutch of 10–15 white oval eggs, usually in a burrow.

GREEN MAMBA
Dendroaspis angusticeps

A regular resident of the roofs of a variety of buildings, including outhouses.
DESCRIPTION 190cm (6ft). The body colour is normally green with a hint of gold between the scales; sometimes the whole body may be of a yellow hue. Like the black mamba it has a long, angular head, but the lining of the mouth is white.
DISTRIBUTION Throughout much of East Africa below the Sahara and down to the Cape in the south.

HABITAT An arboreal snake, shy and rarely seen in its preferred habitat of well-forested areas, but more regularly encountered in the sparser vegetation of dry bush areas and coastal scrub.
FOOD Venomous, feeding almost exclusively on birds and mammals.
BREEDING Up to 10 eggs are laid in a tree hollow or in leaf litter.

BANDED KRAIT
Bungarus fasciatus

Extremely toxic, but so disinclined to bite that Malayan villagers believe it is not a venomous species.
DESCRIPTION Up to 2 metres (6½ft) in size. It has black and yellow cross bands along its entire length.
DISTRIBUTION India and the Malay archipelago.
HABITAT Forests, plantations and farms, where it hides during the day in burrows under stones or logs, becoming active at night.
FOOD Like all kraits other snakes are the preferred food.
BREEDING The female lays eggs.

VIPERS (Family *Viperidae*)

About 190 species. Arguably the most advanced snakes, a group which includes the rattlesnakes, the European Adder (*Vipera berus*) (page 73), and the Gaboon Viper (*Bitis gabonica*) (page 69), which holds the record for length of fangs. This is possible because, as in all vipers, the fangs can be folded into the roof of the mouth and are swivelled forward during a bite. Sometimes the pit vipers (rattlesnakes and their kin) are placed in a separate family. All of them have a heat-sensitive pit on each side of their face, for detecting the body warmth of mammals or birds, enabling them to strike accurately in pitch darkness.

FER-DE-LANCE
Bothrops atrox

More correctly known as Barba Amarilla, this snake has a virulent venom and is reputedly responsible for the most snake-bite related deaths in South America of any species. The true fer-de-lance occurs only on the island of Martinique.

DESCRIPTION Averages 2 metres (6½ft). One of its many common names refers to it as a "lancehead"; its triangular head with light stripes behind the eyes produces an arrow point marking towards the snout. Mostly some shade of brown with darker brown triangles radiating off the back.

DISTRIBUTION From Mexico down through Brazil.

HABITAT Found in plantations and forest, especially along streams.

FOOD Venomous, feeding on small mammals and birds, frogs and lizards.

BREEDING A large female can produce an astonishing litter of up to 70 young measuring 30cm (12in).

GABOON VIPER
Bitis gabonica

This large viper has massive fangs of up to 5cm (2in), a record for any snake. The fangs are folded against the roof of the mouth, but are raised and extended when the snake goes to strike.

DESCRIPTION The largest and fattest of the puff adders at up to 1.8 metres (6ft) and 12kgs (26lb). Very heavy-bodied, with a wide head and silvery eye marked out by a triangle of brown or black extending from the jaw. The colours of the amazingly cryptic body pattern range from brown, beige, yellow, black and purple.

DISTRIBUTION Much of eastern, central and western Africa.

HABITAT Found on the floors of rain forests and woodland, its remarkable patterning camouflages it wonderfully in leaf litter.

FOOD Venomous, eating a variety of terrestrial species, including some birds and, exceptionally, the small royal antelope.

BREEDING Live-bearing, up to 60 young in a litter.

PUFF ADDER
Bitis arietans

Male puff adders may be seen performing strange ritualized combats or dances together during the breeding season.

DESCRIPTION A very heavy-bodied snake, perhaps only 1 metre (3–4ft), but extremely variable in colour, ranging from yellow-brown through reddish brown or grey with heavy black markings.

DISTRIBUTION Africa south of the Sahara, southwest Arabia and Yemen.

HABITAT Most active at night, but in fact generally an ambush feeder, waiting for its prey to pass its silent, camouflaged form. Usually hisses very loudly when threatened.

FOOD Venomous, eating mainly rodents which are quickly digested with the aid of the tissue-destroying nature of the venom.

BREEDING Able to produce massive litters of over 80 live offspring.

CANTIL SNAKE
Agkistrodon bilineatus

The newly hatched young are able to attract their prey by using extraordinary movements of their bright yellow tail lure.

DESCRIPTION A blue-back to chocolate brown snake, with creamy-white markings taking the form of two narrow lateral stripes and regular thin cross bars.

DISTRIBUTION Through much of southern Mexico, Guatemala, El Salvador, Nicaragua,

Honduras and Belize.

HABITAT Mainly nocturnal, it generally resides near water.

FOOD Venomous, feeding on amphibians, fish, mammals and reptiles.

BREEDING Live-bearing, giving birth to over a dozen young.

CANTIL SNAKE

HORNED DESERT VIPER
Cerastes cerastes

A snake of shifting sands that moves by "sidewinding".

DESCRIPTION Average length is about 60cm (2ft). The colour of the snake generally matches the sand surface in the region an individual occurs, varying between pink and yellow, with regular blotching on the back and heavily keeled scales. The most remarkable features are the long horns over the eye that allow sand to accumulate while keeping the eye clear of cover as the snake waits in ambush.

DISTRIBUTION Through much of North Africa and well into the Sahara, to the Middle East.

HABITAT This snake avoids the extremes of desert temperatures by burying itself along the length of its body with rhythmic muscle contractions, then waits for suitable prey to pass by.

FOOD Venomous, feeding on desert rodents and lizards.

BREEDING Lays a clutch of eggs in disused burrows or under stones.

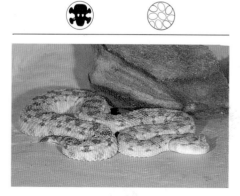

MALAYAN PIT VIPER
Enhydris plumbea

Locally known as the "axe snake" because a bite can have the same result as a blow from an axe – the loss of a limb.
DESCRIPTION Averages 70–80cm (28–32in). Patterned with angular markings of dark brown, edged with black on a reddish-brown background.
DISTRIBUTION Indo-China, Malaya, Sumatra and Borneo.
HABITAT Forests and oil palm plantations where it is particularly common. A perfectly camouflaged "sit and wait" hunter that lies motionless even when approached. Very dangerous to "rubber tappers" if they work without shoes.
FOOD Rodents, frogs and reptiles.
BREEDING After laying 13 to 30 eggs, the female coils around them until they hatch about 40 days later. It is unusual for vipers to show maternal care like this.

ADDER
Vipera berus

The adder has the greatest terrestrial range of any snake in the world.
DESCRIPTION Usually up to 65cm (2ft) but occasionally up to 90cm (3ft). The ground colour is most commonly grey but may be reddish brown, yellow, olive or greenish. It is most easily distinguished by the dark zigzag pattern running down the back and by the dark V or X shaped mark on the head.
DISTRIBUTION Most of Europe (absent from Ireland, southern Spain, Italy and the southern Balkans) up to the Arctic Circle, east to the northern Pacific coast of China.
HABITAT Very varied, moors, woodland, marshy meadows; it is even a capable swimmer.
FOOD Venomous. It eats small mammals and lizards.
BREEDING Live-bearing; litters vary between 4–12 according to the size of the female.

OTTOMAN VIPER
Vipera xanthina

This snake can be distinguished from the other vipers in its European range, as it is the only one that lacks a nose horn.
DESCRIPTION Up to 120cm (4ft). Thick-bodied with no nose horn or characteristic head pattern. The colour is variable, grey, sandy or darker, with pronounced eye stripe and a mark on the mouth just under the eye. The dark brown stripe on the back is irregular, often broken up into blotches; the underside is greyish, but yellow or orange under the tail.
DISTRIBUTION Turkey, through Asia Minor into Lebanon and the ex-Soviet Union.
HABITAT Found in open woodland, rocky hillsides, pastures and often cultivated areas. A sluggish viper, diurnal normally, but can be active at night during the hotter months.
FOOD Venomous with a bite that could be fatal to human beings. Feeds mainly on mammals and birds but may take lizards also.

BREEDING Live-bearing, averaging around 15 in a litter.

COPPERHEAD
Agkistrodon contortrix

Though painful, the venomous bite of the copperhead rarely causes fatalities.
DESCRIPTION 61–134cm (2–4½ft). Usually a fairly chunky snake. Often distinguished by a coppery-red head and a classic hourglass pattern across the back that is dark brown on the tan, orange or greyish ground colour. A pit viper, it has small facial pits; the body scales are weakly keeled.
DISTRIBUTION Much of southeastern USA, except Florida, and bounded in the west by central Texas and Kansas.

HABITAT Found in a variety of habitats from rocky hillsides to lush swamp vegetation, its coloration makes it inconspicuous, but if disturbed it will vibrate its tail rapidly and will strike swiftly.
FOOD Venomous, eating mainly small mammals, but also lizards, snakes, amphibians and insects such as cicadas.
BREEDING Live-bearing; the young have bright yellow tail-tips that fade as the snake ages.

NOSE-HORNED VIPER
Vipera ammodytes

Highly venomous, potentially the most dangerous viper in Europe.
DESCRIPTION Up to 90cm (3ft) long, but more regularly under 65cm (2ft). Stout-bodied with a triangular head, males are more often grey and females browner. A clearly marked zigzag striping is normally unbroken on the back, while the underside is greyish to pink with some darker spotting and red, yellow or green under the tail.
DISTRIBUTION A southern species, from

northern Italy through the Balkans into Greece and South West Asia.
HABITAT Prefers dry, sunny, rocky slopes with some vegetation. Mostly terrestrial, but can climb; usually encountered during the day and when disturbed hisses loudly.
FOOD Venomous. Feeds mostly on small mammals, birds and lizards.
BREEDING The females bear live young, which are born in late summer.

NOSE-HORNED VIPER

COTTONMOUTH
Agkistrodon piscivorus

This dangerous snake will often give warning when disturbed by vibrating its tail and gaping its mouth to reveal the "cotton"-white interior.
DESCRIPTION 76–189cm (2½–6ft). A large snake that is dark, olive, brown or black above. The cross banding on the back is darker still, but sometimes hard to see, while the belly is usually a little lighter than the back. Care is needed to distinguish it from water snakes, but the presence of facial pits and (on a dead specimen) the single anal scale are diagnostic.
DISTRIBUTION The southeastern states of the USA, from Virginia in an arc bounded by the eastern seaboard taking in Florida through to Oklahoma and Texas.
HABITAT Semi-aquatic, found in swamps, lakes and ditches. A fairly lethargic snake whose behaviour in retreating slowly or standing its ground when disturbed marks it out from the fast-fleeing water snakes, as does its habit of vibrating its tail.

FOOD Venomous, mainly feeding on fish, but will take birds, mammals and amphibians, as well as baby alligators and turtles.
BREEDING Live-bearing; gives birth between August and September to up to 15 young. Breeds mainly every other year.

SIDEWINDER
Crotalus cerastes

Famous for its classic mode of locomotion that never allows too much of the body to touch the burning desert surface at any one time.
DESCRIPTION 43–82cm (1½–2½ft). A shortish, stubby rattlesnake with prominently rough scales and triangular horns over the eyes.
DISTRIBUTION Northwestern Mexico, southern parts of Utah, Arizona, Nevada and eastern California.
HABITAT Spends the day hidden in mammal burrows or beneath low bushes; it emerges into its arid desert habitat mainly at night. Often encountered basking at the side of roads during the day; otherwise elusive, but the parallel J shaped markings it makes in the sand are a distinctive sign of its presence in an area.
FOOD Venomous; eats pocket mice, kangaroo rats and lizards.
BREEDING Live-bearing, producing 5–18 young in late summer or early autumn.

TIMBER RATTLESNAKE
Crotalus horridus

The only rattlesnake in most of northeastern USA, but relatively common only in undisturbed montane areas as it has been persecuted in much of the rest of its range.
DESCRIPTION 88–189cm (3–6ft). Large variation between southern and northern populations. The head may be unmarked or with a dark stripe behind the eye, the back may be dark with blotches on the side and forming cross bands nearer the tail or it may have a brownish stripe running down it with chevron-like cross banding. Both show a black tail.
DISTRIBUTION Much of eastern USA, from Maine south to northern Florida, west into Minnesota and Texas.

HABITAT Prefers remote areas, wooded hillsides, rock outcrops, swamps and river floodplains. Active between April and October, mostly during daylight but also at night during the summer. In October the snakes may congregate in great numbers at favoured hibernation sites.
FOOD Venomous; often waiting perfectly still in order to ambush prey such as squirrels, chipmunks, mice and birds.
BREEDING Females give birth every other year, producing 5–17 live-born young between late August to October.

TIMBER RATTLESNAKE

WESTERN RATTLESNAKE
Crotalus viridis

One of the most aggressive of the rattlesnakes, its bite can be lethal even if treated.
DESCRIPTION 40–162cm (1½–5½ft). Very variable over much of its range, but often with two diagonal stripes on the head, one above and one below the eye. It is mainly some shade of brown with darker, regular blotches on the back and sides that thin nearer the tail and almost join to become bands. The lighter coloured tail is ringed with black at the base.
DISTRIBUTION Much of western USA, into northern Mexico and some southern parts of western Canada.
HABITAT Mainly crepuscular, preferring rock canyons and scrubby slopes, but often found in agricultural and suburban locations.
FOOD Venomous, preying chiefly on small rodents.
BREEDING 4–21 live-born young are produced from August to October, after mating either in autumn or in March or May.

WESTERN DIAMONDBACK RATTLESNAKE
Crotalus atrox

Noted for its defensive position when it raises its head well above the coils in a classic S shaped pose and intermittently compounds its threat by rattling its tail.
DESCRIPTION 86–213cm (3–7ft). A large snake with variable coloration, usually brownish with pale-bordered diamond-shape patches on the back. The tail is ringed with black and white bands.
DISTRIBUTION Southwestern USA and into northern Mexico.

HABITAT Prefers dry or semi-arid areas like canyons and scrubby plains, but also montane locations and river bluffs. A secretive snake, but one that is often in close proximity to areas of human population and is annually persecuted in the "rattlesnake round-ups".
FOOD Venomous, feeding on rodents and birds.
BREEDING 4–25 young are live-born in late summer.

BLACK-TAILED RATTLESNAKE
Crotalus molossus

Possibly the rattlesnake that is least likely to rattle when disturbed.
DESCRIPTION 71–125cm (2–4ft). The body colour varies from greyish-brown to a very impressive yellow-brown. The markings on the back are inevitably darker than the ground colour and with paler centres; they form diamonds nearer the head and thick bands towards the tail. The pattern is usually edged in white or grey and the tail is plain black.
DISTRIBUTION From Arizona, east into central Texas and south into northern Mexico.
HABITAT Found on cliffs and rock outcrops, often near streams, but also encountered in pine and deciduous woodland.
FOOD Venomous, feeds on a variety of small rodents.
BREEDING 3–6 live-born young are born in late summer.

MASSASAUGA
Sistrurus catenatus

Differs from all other rattlers by having 9 large scales at the front of the head.

DESCRIPTION At only up to 100cm (40in), a short, but well-proportioned, snake. A light grey to grey-brown snake with a row of large brown, grey or black blotches down the back and smaller and fainter spots on the side. Has a broad dark eye stripe and a long mark from the head to the neck, sometimes shaped like a lyre.

DISTRIBUTION Southern Canada (Ontario), southwest to Arizona and northeastern Mexico.

HABITAT Prefers moist situations like swamps and around rivers, but in the west it adapts to drier conditions.

FOOD Venomous, eating lizards, snakes, small mammals and frogs.

BREEDING Live-bearing; a litter of 2–19 is born between July and September.

INDEX